Nobody 101

A Loser's Guide to Life

Marlaina Donato

Ekstasis Multimedia
Lakeville, Pennsylvania

Ekstasis Multimedia: www.booksandbrush.net

Nobody 101/Marlaina Donato
Lakeville, Pennsylvania: Ekstasis Multimedia, 2015
ISBN-13: 978-0692465363
ISBN-10: 0692465367

Cover art: Albert H. Davis
Cover design: Marlaina Donato
Interior art: Marlaina Donato
*with the exception of public domain images

The Nobody Blues from the book Impatient Purity by Winifred Druhan (Ekstasis Multimedia, 2013)

For the Belching Bimbos, Charlie and Ignats, and the Grande Hotel.

CONTENTS

The Nobody Blues

Fill your gut, drink your fill.
Go to bed, take your pill.
Take a walk, feel the cold cement.
Smell the fumes, pay the rent.
Manicure the blistered hands.
Wipe the sweat, put on the fans.
Shovel the snow, slip on the ice.
Try to escape
'Til your brain's in a vice.
Take a vacation, get a disease
Then you won't feel guilty
For having some ease.
Maybe tomorrow you can live today-
Your day off could fall
On a sunny day!

-Winifred Druhan

INTRODUCTION

To quote Emily Dickinson, "I'm Nobody, who are you?"

Yup, I'm Nobody and proud of it. I've been kicked around, not listened to, taken advantage of, discredited and underestimated all my life. And that's just some of the good stuff. You know how I feel. You've dreamed of making a difference, getting on top, telling the world off. You have hernias to prove how hard you tried to help yourself. But there was always that Somebody who pushed you out of line and got there first.

Well, like most Charlie Browns of the world, we just keep plugging and making asses out of ourselves. Then one day we wake up and realize it's time to make some changes.

There's a difference between being a nobody and a Nobody. A nobody stays in the sewer and thrives on being a sympathy sucker. However, a Nobody (with a proud capital "N") uses his or her status. A Nobody can say just about anything and get away with it because no one cares anyway. A Nobody can speak for all of the other nobodies who need a voice.

Okay, I got out of bed this morning thinking that maybe if I was Somebody, I could write a book that would miraculously change the world. So, as a Nobody, I sat down to write a book that would miraculously change my own life. Again to quote Emily Dickinson, "The soul selects her own society then shuts the door..." Why don't you come along with me? Nobodies are the backbone of society. We might as well make it our own.

Jesus of Nazareth. Sir Isaac Newton. Albert Einstein. Walt Whitman. Susan B. Anthony. Helen Keller. Martin Luther King, Jr. John Lennon. William Shakespeare. Oprah Winfrey. Morris the Cat. Just to name a few Nobodies who became Somebodies. Remember the company we keep. Lives are meant to be dreamed; dreams are meant to be lived.

MARRYING THE BUS DRIVER

In case you just came in, I'll
reintroduce myself. I'm Nobody
from Nowhere, USA. You see, the
best part of being a Nobody is the
potential factor. If you have hidden
genius, everyone ignores you. If you
don't, everyone ignores you anyway.

Either way you win, and there's no pressure to succeed. This means that when you finally make it you have the sublime pleasure of watching all of the Muttfaces who joined the Trash Your Dream Club get whiplash from disbelief. And when you fall flat on your face, no one is disappointed.

I've been there. The flat-on-your-face place, I mean. The only whiplashing and disbelieving going on here lately has been in my mirror, but that's okay.

Nobody 101: Every Underdog gets his day.

Prove it, you say? Just look at any Somebody who earned their status. Look really hard and close.

Between the lines of every notable biography you can see the doubting Muttfaces slink out with their tails between their legs.

Speaking of Muttfaces. Just last week, here in Nowhere, USA. a local man suffered a severe injury to the head from reading a book. The man started to feel dizzy after reading the first few paragraphs but ignored his symptoms. After experiencing nausea, headache, and breathlessness, he felt a tremendous blow to his brain and then fell unconscious. You get the picture. Even Bruce Springsteen couldn't dream up a town this insulting to a mildly intelligent Nobody/aspiring Somebody. Heck, anyone wearing glasses and carrying a book is considered armed and dangerous.

Alright, enough Muttface bashing. They can't help if they are horizon-challenged and their only goal is to find toilet paper with instructions. We have more important things to do.

Nobody 101: Even Muttfaces contribute to our success. They make us want more.

Yeah, like me, I bet your garbage-eating addiction has gotten you into one problem after another. Now, this is where the bus driver comes in. If you are a Nobody with considerable Somebody potential, you've probably been shipwrecked with the following adjectives since kindergarten:

crazy

lazy

weird

stupid

The worst part of these adjectives is the nouns they have for neighbors:

airhead

cloudhead

dreamer

near-do-well

lard ass

After a while, most of us Nobodies begin to sympathize with the Muttface popular vote. This means that the first person who shows us any kind of validation becomes a deity. You remember that drooling kid in school who had a crush on you and you went "out" together just because he/she was the only other human alive to acknowledge your existence... Some of us Nobodies remember sucking up to just about anyone who didn't give us a black eye.

That's how the pattern begins- the pattern of irrational gratitude. Okay, it's perfectly decent to appreciate what people do for us. Almost everyone we meet, positive or negative, has some effect on our lives. But just because the bus driver gets you to your destination doesn't mean you have to marry him. If we do, we end up schlepping a hundred bus drivers through life.

Nobody 101: Know when to let go of outgrown attitudes, beliefs, keepsakes, cars, belongings and relationships.

Then there's the other side of the coin. Some people think **we're** the bus driver. Every now and then, a person recognizes our Somebody potential. Some are on the level while others are hyenas in VIP suits. Unfortunately, "friends" can also be hyenas. You know the drill. You do all of the calling, talking, supporting, inquiring, comforting, uplifting and emotional wet-nursing; however, when you are standing on the ledge in front of a crowd chanting "Jump!" your so-called friends are selling hot dogs and charging admission to watch your knickers fly off on the way down.

16

Or the other variety of friendly hyena; they give you a crumb of friendship but keep you at arm's length because to have you any closer would give their ego panic attacks. You know the ones...they invite you over for lunch once in a decade and sneak you in the back door. They're smart hyenas; they keep you in their back pocket just in case you become a Somebody.

Nobody 101: Select your free rides carefully.

Some of us nobodies, if we're lucky, happen to meet at least one great soul during the journey. This can be a true friend, lover, family member, or an animal companion. You will recognize them immediately. They give us roots so we can reach into heaven with full hands. They give us rain when our spirits are in drought. They give us sun and rejoice when we bear fruit. These great souls nurture our lives and accompany us from seed to harvest. These are the ones who earn to share the banquet with us.

Nobody 101: There are good people out there. Don't give up until you find one and then don't screw it up.

I say "don't screw it up" because I've known plenty of Nobodies who became so disillusioned with the world that when someone or something really good came along, they wouldn't allow themselves to trust it.

This reminds me of a stray cat I once observed. He was a tattered, gray veteran of the streets, scarred and definitely a Nobody with Somebody potential. You could tell he was beautiful once, and still could be with some care. Every day he would take food from the same house where an elderly lady lived. Year after year, she left food out, and he'd eat and nap on her front step. But despite all effort from the lady upstairs, the cat refused to make further contact. One day we locked eyes. The creature's expression was that of total defeat, despair, and perhaps, something akin to what we humans experience as rage. The saddest thing about this feline was not his obvious lot in life but the fact that he was home and didn't know it. His innocence and trust had been so profoundly scarred that he could no longer recognize a safe place or a safe heart.

Often, Nobodies are like flowers without thorns. They end up worn down to the stem. When we can no longer tolerate people pulling our petals out, something deep inside us rises up. Eureka! We start getting thorns and learn how to protect what is most important in our lives. But we have to be cautious. A few thorns can protect us; too many can keep out the beauty and love that make life worth living for.

All creatures have defense mechanisms such as fangs, venom, camouflage, speed, claws, wings, toxins, bright colors, vocal displays, and rattling tails. Human beings are no different except for the fact that emotional baggage, ego, and an innate appetite for evil can cloud the motive for our defenses. Sure, there are savage killers in the animal world, but these killers usually kill for survival not because the victim is wearing two hundred dollar sneakers.

So, if you are like the majority of Nobodies, you probably had to acquire a defense, something other people are naturally born with. This may take some time. Nobodies have very low bottoms. Sometimes

Nobodies don't acquire any defense. They just eat enough dung until one day they blow up the post office and we see them on the news. "But he was so nice!" people say, "He wouldn't hurt a fly!"

Case in point. You and I know how nice he was. So nice he had shit coming out of his ears. But blowing up buildings is not the solution (just in case it crossed your mind today). The only way to prevent such a tragedy is to set personal boundaries and release the anger in a healthy way.

If you are like me, you are probably a walking stew—stew as in soup. That's right, your fourth grade teacher, your mother-in-law, your ex-lover, your boss from ten years ago, and your long-dead landlord are all simmering in their juices inside your gut. The only antidote is not adding another person to it.

Next time you are confronted with a bully, get if off your chest. If getting it off your chest means compromising your job, the roof over your head, or your relationship, then find a way to set boundaries that will also keep the peace. Keeping peace does not mean you have to be a dung-eating doormat but acting and speaking with everyone's wellbeing in mind, including your own.

Like I said, animals know what they are doing. The other day I noticed a small band of deer outside my window. I usually see them just before nightfall, nibbling their way up the hill. This time I noticed a particularly lovely doe. She waited patiently for the others to catch up with her, touching noses with the first. The second and third siblings rejected her and it seemed to have a profound effect on the young deer. Apparently, they were too hungry to nuzzle or they decided she needed a breath mint. She looked at them and waited. Stared. Gracefully stomped her hoof. Finally, she put her ears back. That's when I knew she meant business. She looked in the opposite direction and then at her siblings. Suddenly, she bolted. That's right, left the rest of them in shock. All five remaining doe froze mid-mouthful and watched her bound through the woods. Two minutes passed by before they all chalked up her behavior to temperamental youth.

I figured if a deer can get pissed off and do something about it, so can I.

Nobody 101: We all have an inborn right to put our ears back and make our feelings known.

Closing thought: remember the rattlesnake. Yeah, he's an ornery son-of-a-bitch, but he warns you first. Next time someone has their boot on your neck, rattle like hell. If the boot doesn't take heed, you know the drill.

And next time **you** have your face where it doesn't belong and you hear a rattle, run like hell.

WHY DIDN'T THE CHICKEN CROSS THE ROAD?

Because he was chicken. And a nobody (notice the lower case "n"). If he was an upper case Nobody, he would have crossed anyway. Bravery doesn't mean there is an absence of fear, only the presence of determination. Guts, nerve, chutzpah, balls—whatever you call it--is what separates the nobodies from the Nobodies and what turns Nobodies into Somebodies. Every great person has it. Ants have it. Mountain goats have it. Your toddler who keeps trying to unlock the kiddie gate has it. It helps if you're born with it, but if you're not, don't fret. It can be acquired.

How? Find your passion. What inspires a person to tolerate, even adore, a lover's obnoxious habits? Passion! What enables an expecting mother to cope with the challenges of pregnancy? Passion! What inspires a budding guitarist to withstand bleeding fingertips?

Passion! We are all capable of feeling passion, that euphoria, that rush that makes all work, pain, and frustration worth the darn trouble.

Nobody 101: Make passion your fuel.

But there is only one thing that can plunge passion into ice water, and that's fear. Fear of failure. Fear of success. Fear of rejection. Fear of real love. Fear of the true Self.

But we have a choice. We can be like the chicken who was a ninny and didn't cross the road or risk being roadkill for our dreams. If we make it to the other side, great. If not, no prob. Swallowing fear insures us nine lives.

Unfortunately, some Nobodies eat,

sleep, dream, and marry fear. I once knew a young woman who was so scared on her wedding night that she stepped into the hot tub with her nightgown on. To say the least, it took a while before the honeymoon started. When I was eight years old, a neighbor called our house at ten o'clock at night and asked my father if he'd come over and kill the spider on her wall. I was also terrified of spiders, but the woman's request sent me into belly-aching laughter.

Only today I can see how sad it is when fear like this drags us through life by the neck. If you're like the rest of us, you probably have a few nightgowns, hot tubs, and spiders in your fear closet, too. Some Nobodies hoard fears, collecting them into neat, little piles until life becomes like an obstacle course. Fear gives us false contentment. We can get so accustomed to the prison we create for ourselves that venturing beyond it is terrifying. So why are Nobodies self-proclaimed convicts? It goes back to the chicken. The meekest, weakest, and weirdest chicken in the pen gets pecked to death. It is a fact of life. Pick, peck, pick. We're pecked until we're bald Nobodies.

Speaking of bald. The great composer Beethoven is a prime example. During his lifetime, he suffered heartbreak, ill health, deafness, and isolation. Many misunderstood him or were recipients of his acquired defenses. By the time of his death, his reputation was not pristine, but even his haters gathered around his casket to claim a strand of hair for profit or a macabre souvenir. Either way, the genius went to his grave bald.

Sometimes it is human nature to want to destroy what it loves and love what it hates. And it is human nature for Nobodies to learn to hate themselves. Nobodies who begin life with shyness, low self-esteem, sensitivity, or challenges are magnets for Muttfaces who have never known a shy, passive or sick day in their lives. When you are used to nothing but black eyes (literal or metaphorical), invisibility, ridicule or isolation, it is very easy to fall in love with the dark angel, Fear. But instead of following it into Hell, we can learn from it. Fear can be an angel because it can teach us which person, place, and thing is poison to our potential and our well- being.

If we're not careful, fear can also make us just like the Muttfaces. As a child, after being ridiculed for years for a stammer, I finally made some friends after moving and going to a new school. I was no longer an amoeba and desperate to keep my promotion. There was one girl who was not only a meek chicken but a very skinny chicken, and she became the hen-peck of the day. She was my friend until other kids teased me for wanting to hang around with her. I not only went along with the Muttfaces but became one of them. I got stomachaches from guilt. The fear of being demoted outweighed my nature to stick up for the underdog.

One day, after the girl looked at me heartbroken and ran out of the classroom sobbing, I realized my own cruelty. Thankfully, her grace of heart enabled her to forgive my horrid behavior, and my Muttface days came to an end. In case I never officially apologized, Sandy, if

you're reading this, I'm sorry. I hope
you finally got chicken audacity and
crossed the road, and you are a big
Somebody.

Nobody 101: Fear can uncover our greatest strengths if we use it to our advantage.

Just as fear can uncover our
greatest assets, it can also throw
the spotlight on our greatest
weakness—negative ego. I preface
the word "ego" with the word
"negative" because there is also
such a thing called positive ego.
The little train "that could" in your
childhood book had positive ego. He
knew he could do it, told himself he
could, and he did. That's positive
ego. It's the tiny voice inside our
Nobody brains that assures us of

our capabilities and blesses us with resilience when the hills in our lives defeat our huffing and puffing. Now, we wouldn't call the train an ego maniac because he knew his destiny, would we?

Negative ego is different and grows on fear like fungus. It eats up all reasoning and self-esteem and turns a person into an Ego Addict. You know Ego Addicts. They don't leave home without it and their business cards read, "Have ego, will travel." They burn two thousand calories a minute and are hunched over from schlepping their egos through town. They're like dung beetles; their only goal is to stir up the shit wherever they go.

Hindus call the breath of life *prana*. After you spend some time with an Ego Addict, you'll know you've been bled dry of it. You see, Ego Addicts are Prana Suckers. They suck, snort, inhale and devour your sympathy, patience, love, understanding, favors, and hopes like psychic vacuum cleaners. After a single conversation (often one-sided) with a Prana Sucker, you end up feeling like the undead.

Unfortunately, Nobodies wittingly or unwittingly send out engraved invitations, roll out the red carpet and wine and dine Prana Suckers. We're experts. We're magnets. We're diehards. But we're not gonna take it anymore. From now on, we're on Prana Sucker strike.

Next time you see the anteaters heading your way, know they're having a bad ego day but you don't have to fix it, take it, or authorize being sucked up.

Nobody 101: Don't get sucked in! If it's *your* ego, stop suckin'.

Muttfaces, Ego Addicts, Prana Suckers, Trash Your Dream associates are synonyms for very scared people. The more of them you have in your life, the more you've got what it takes to be a Somebody. At their worst, they cripple your self-esteem if you let them. At their most harmless, they make a Nobody's life interesting. Without every Muttface, Ego

Addict, Prana Sucker, and Trash Your Dream associate I've ever known, this book (and many others) would not have been possible. Every garden needs compost.

ONE HEADLIGHT and A SACRED COW

Ego and all the prana-sucking habits that accompany it lead us to the next topic—humility. Humility is not what makes a person a dung-eater nor is it an antidote to negative ego. Humility is a state of being that leaves no room for arrogance.

Arrogance makes a person think that he or she is so superior, so indispensable, so important that he thinks he can tame nature; that there are no other life forms in the universe beside his glorious kind; that he can't piss without using his cell phone. Unfortunately, every human on the planet has arrogance floating in his bloodstream like a dormant virus. The worst part about it is that is spreads faster than gossip churned up by the Muttfaces.

Take some average, infected humans. After they cut down acres of trees to build one house, they plant new ones for decoration. They must wear alien-looking, protective gear when they spray crops with chemical pesticides but think it is perfectly fine to eat what is being sprayed. They think every ditch by the side of the road is a convenient trash bin, compliments of Mother Nature. They don't believe in any person, place, or thing that they haven't seen personally or hasn't actually bitten them in the behind. After they laugh on the way to the bank, eat a good meal, placate their genitals and snore away a good eight hours, they refuse to acknowledge the possibility that there might be another purpose to life. After knowing that life forms on this planet are still being discovered and that some may never be discovered, the theory of additional life in the universe is ludicrous to them. They uphold decent, honorable and even religious character yet are capable of cruelty because someone else's God looks different than their own.

Now, if you were one of those little gray guys in a spaceship, wouldn't you want to dissect him, too?

As Nobodies, humility is a very good thing to have. It helps us to see ourselves with an objective eye. Humility allows us to be gardeners so we can pull out weeds of bad character, prune back destructive habits and be content with the fact that we all bloom in our own time.

Humility blesses us with a few sacred cows. Sacred cows give us reason to get out of bed in the morning. Who cares if Professor Thinks-He-Knows-It-All says that a Higher Power, aliens, souls and the emotions of animals don't exist? Whoever plays Gods by discarding someone else's is not only a hypocrite but a Muttface in the first degree.

Nobody 101: Sometimes not having all the answers is answer enough.

Humility gives us the ability to recover from our mistakes gracefully. It not only inspires us to never stop learning but reminds us that we can learn something from anyone and anything. Even headlights. Let me explain.

You see, if you lived in Nowhere, USA, in the ten minutes that it takes to drive to the store for a loaf of bread, you would probably count eight cars with only one headlight. One night I counted so many that I found myself getting a little paranoid. *Maybe it's an underground Muttface cult and they're taking over!* I thought. Cult or no cult, the one headlight thing eventually activated the dreadful Arrogance Virus within my own psyche.

I had two working headlights on **my** car. It went to my head. After about a year of yelling out Muttface insults to passing cars, one night I found it very difficult to drive. I figured I was tired. Then it happened another night. I figured the headlights must be dirty. After the third night, I thought I needed glasses. Then it hit me. Could it be? Never! Hell would freeze over before *I* would have a car with only one working headlight.

Well, folks, the Devil went ice skating.

Nobody 101: Laugh at yourself, even if it kills you.

That is, without self-judgment. Laughter keeps the Arrogance Virus from doing further damage. What a relief it is to finally admit that we're all human. Unfortunately, being human means that no one is or ever will be perfect (my apologies to all of the Muttfaces). Of course, everyone has heard and known this but accepting it is like swallowing poison and asking for seconds.

So, if perfectionism is only a humanmade concept and we know it's only job is to give us ulcers, why do we eternally strive to hit this mythical mark? My personal Nobody belief is that without hunger for perfection, none of us would ever progress. Like flowers, we dream of reaching the sun; we'll never touch it, but we grow trying. Blaze in your perfect imperfection.

Nobody 101: Progress is the only perfection.

This hunger has plunged our society

into an abyss of self-hatred and discontent. Fashion magazines, cosmetic surgeons, psychiatrists, rehabs and eating disorder clinics are thriving on our obsession with a manmade ideal. We follow dogma, ignorance and whims of the media like sheep to the slaughter. What is "acceptable" is subject to the day, month, year, decade and century. This whim-hopping and herd-following has been going on since time began. In the ancient world, women were revered and a feminine God was believed to be in charge. Centuries later, when Orthodox religion and patriarchal rule reigned, women were then believed to not even possess souls. During the Golden Age of Greece, male homosexuality was considered the highest aesthetic while conventional marriage was seen as inferior but necessary to continue the bloodline. Homosexuals of both genders were esteemed in many Tribal cultures and believed that they brought good fortune to the community. Overall, sexual labels were non-existent in the ancient world. Today, many gay people are persecuted, some tied to fences and left to die in the name of someone else's prejudice. Actors were once seen as society's lowest; today, they are nearly deified.

Nobody 101: Refuse to dress, live or love according to the whims of the day.

CLIMBING A MOUNTAIN
ON ROLLER SKATES

It's a fact. Every Nobody can probably remember that defining moment when they realized who they are. It's like your first crush, your first bra or braces. You just never forget it.

My initiation into Nobodyhood took place in the 5th grade. I was nothing but a shy, stammering, classical-music-loving, orange-pants-wearing Muttface target. Even the teachers enjoyed imitating my stutter. One time during class, after I was called on to read aloud, the teacher promptly began to continue the class lessons with an obvious, forced stammer. Of course, the rest of the students saw this as fine entertainment on a Monday morning, and it wasn't long until the room was filled with unrestrained snickering. The teacher enjoyed it so much that he let out a small laugh when he grinned at me. What can a 10-year-old Nobody do? Get revenge, right where it hurts. In the intellect.

We had an assignment to memorize the digestive process in detail and deliver an oral examination. On test day, no one wanted to go first, so I forced my lower case "n" to evolve to an upper case "N". I volunteered. In front of the class, halfway to the small intestine, even my stutter was stuttering. I was shaking. The room was giggling, snickering and whispering. I wanted to run, hide, die and reincarnate. But I finished.

At the end of class, the teacher lectured everyone for doing a pathetic job and then announced that only one student had earned a good grade. An A+. My name was announced; Muttface jaws dropped. At that moment, I thanked the Patron Saint of Losers and savored my small success.

Success. Emily Dickinson says it is "counted sweetest by those who never succeed." Most people equate it with money, power or fame. If this is true, then we could say that this great poet was a failure because she chose a quiet life and kept her body of work for her own eyes and hidden in a drawer. Luckily for us, her work was discovered after her death.

Being a Somebody does not require money or fame, but it does require power. A negative Somebody uses his/her power *over* others. A positive Somebody uses his/her power over *personal limitation.* This is success. Getting up one more day to a job you despise in order to keep your family fed or put yourself through school is success. Getting back on the horse after setbacks is success. Running a marathon despite coming in last is success. Getting an A+ after making an ass out of yourself is success. So you see, you don't have to find a cure for a disease, win an Oscar, swim the Atlantic or build casinos in order to consider yourself successful. If you push beyond your own limitations, fall a million times and die trying, you are a success. If you are loved by a single person, including yourself, you are a success. If you weren't constipated today, you are a success.

Nobody 101: Success does not discriminate.

Let me take a detour for a moment. The other day someone said to me, "It's not nice to call people muttfaces." Allow me to clarify: I am not calling *people* muttfaces. I'm just calling *Muttfaces* muttfaces.

Now, on to roller skates. Nobodies are born wearing them. We pop out of the womb screaming to go places. We are born with an unusual amount of ambition. Yup, we're the toddlers and teenagers from Hell. Trouble is, we want to get where we want to go as quickly as we can conjure it in our brains. Before long, our roller skates meet up with a mountain. This mountain is usually our most treasured dream and desired goal. With the mega balls of a supercharged mountain goat, we attack Mount Everest. We all know what happens next. With spinning wheels we end up nose-first in the dung heap, and that's where we stay unless we do one simple thing: take off the darn roller skates.

Mountains, goals and plans all require one step at a time, not roller skates or pogo sticks. Call it frustrating. Call it karma. But it's the only way to get to the top.

So you climb and climb, crawl and crawl. You've lost your faith six thousand feet ago, your back is broken and your soul is in shreds. That's when you pause. That's right, pause and take a good look around.

Nobody 101: Success is seeing what's already been accomplished, not how far you have to go.

The more your view of the top is limited and obstructed, the higher you are. When you can't see anything at all but the rock face in front of you, the top is closer than ever before.

What if you change your mind and decide it's all too darn hard? Then you have another destiny. You know it's your destiny if you have no other choice but to keep going. Yeah, you might go on mountain strike, yell a lot, curse the gods and invite vultures to your sad sack of bones, but if it's your calling you'll eventually continue on.

This is where it gets a little tricky. A lot of Nobodies charge after a goal that will bring them fame and success and spoon feed crow to the Muttfaces. This is not an authentic mountain. It's a Revenge Mountain. Revenge Mountains can be climbed but once you're up there you still feel like crap. Conquering authentic mountains frees your soul.

Nobody 101: Choose an honest mountain to climb; all others waste your true purpose.

The best revenge is not living well,

as the old saying goes. It is living at peace with yourself.

Then there's a little thing we call luck. Not many people know this, but Lady Luck has an evil twin sister. Most Nobodies meet her; some even shack up with her. Just when the mountain is getting easier to climb and you're starting to enjoy the view, watch out. Just when you're breathing in some accomplishment and feeling happy, she sends a bird over to shit on your head.

You can't see, hear, touch or smell her but there's no mistaking her presence. She's the one who plants a boil in your forehead two hours before that important job interview.

She's the one who makes you run into an ex-lover when you look like a drowned rat. And she's the one who makes the company you work for go bankrupt a year before your retirement. The woman is a bitch, but she has one weakness: she gets bored.

The next time she slithers into your peace of mind, try not to react. Act like you don't give a rat's behind. If she can't get a rise out of you, she moves on. And if you are like the rest of the Nobodies out there, you probably are so used to her antics that you hardly notice her anyway. That's a good sign. It means that Lady Bitch and the Farts (oops, I mean Fates) will soon be moving

60

on. If they can't play with you, they're outta here.

Nobody 101: Nothing lasts forever. It's the law of life.

Many Nobodies are creative souls, and many Nobodies can probably relate to a very prevalent but barely-acknowledged phenomenon called Arm's Length Disorder. There isn't a drug for it but there should be.

Are you a Nobody who just created a new painting? Written a book? Composed a song? Nailed that audition? And the person you tell checks out of the conversation? Maybe even the friendship? Yup, I figured. First the eyes go blank. Then if you're lucky, the other person changes the topic of conversation as quickly as a hawk can snatch up a rodent. If you're not so lucky, dead silence prevails until you wonder if you need to put a mirror under the person's nose or offer subtitles.

A.L.D. affects acquaintances, strangers, friends and even family. If you know them a long time, you'll notice contact dwindling and affection cooling under the umbrella excuse of "I'm so busy!" Those afflicted with A.L.D. can sometimes act like vampires in the presence of garlic.

Nobody 101: Don't apologize for seeing through bullshit.

Wanna clear a room of A.L.D. sufferers? Just announce some wonderful news that has anything to do with something they can't relate to or envy. Arm's Length Disorder can come upon even the most loyal supporters which can give us whiplash from wondering what happened. Until one day we accept the sad fact that A.L.D. goes with the territory. As Nobodies, we've taken a lot in life, but it is never easy to admit that people we love without a clause in the contract can be so utterly and subtly cruel.

Nobody 101: (to quote a fortune cookie) Keep your goals away from the trolls.

Creations are offspring; each goes through gestation and birth, some of them long and agonizing. To the creator, it is not okay when something precious is blatantly dismissed, trashed or ignored. If creations were living, breathing children, it would be unthinkable in our society to do to them what some people do to our creative efforts.

If you are a Nobody who has lived long enough and are beginning to feel at home in your own skin, you probably have earned enough self-esteem to recognize the many shades of jealousy out there. Muttfaces stay up nights figuring out how to get you in the Achilles' heel. The only antidote to jealousy is to know that you must be doing something right.

Nobody 101: We were never meant to play small so someone else can feel bigger.

SINKING SHIPS and DUCT TAPE

If you're a typical, open-hearted, sensitive Nobody, you must have gone through at least one affair of the heart that left you with Post Traumatic Stress Disorder. Bad love affairs, unrequited debacles, fleeting fancies, scandalous passions and heated flirtations are all in our Nobody closets. Some of them actually happen while others remain dead-bolted in our fantasies. Either way, those around us are left to shake their heads and surmise we're not tied too tight. For us, falling in love—or crashing into unrequited love—is as life-altering as an amputation. But let's face it. We're in a half-hearted world where love—to everyone else—is often nothing more than an annoying hangnail.

Most Nobodies survive break-ups with the grace of a 747 crashing into a mountain. Our concerned loved ones leave the house by prefacing, "Now you wouldn't do anything stupid, would you?" as their eyes scan the room for any sharp objects or poisonous substances. Apparently, our Nobody depth of feeling and tendency to court melodrama gives people the false impression that we must have nothing left to live for once the lover we thought was a rose turns out to be a Venus flytrap. Nobodies make good snacks for such toxic creatures, and the only antidote is realizing that Cupid can be a good con artist.

On the way to this insight, we might stay up nights telling our exes off in our minds, thinking of brilliant comebacks to their snarky barbs that left us tongue-tied in the moment. We dream of buying every package of duct tape in the store and wrapping their mouths with it.

If we don't put all of this fitful creativity to good use, we can waste years of solid potential. If we take our cue from the masters, a broken heart can be the driving force behind great creative work. It sure beats getting drunk, taking to our beds or discovering the nearest bakery and waddling out only after we've gained 20 pounds.

We're living in a time when anyone who eats a can of beans and farts through a tube of paint is seen as a gifted artist. Imagine if all of the talented Nobodies of the world crawled into the mud of their own anguish and found a blooming lotus? Imagine if we all faced our own mess and created something beautiful with this rich, fertile soil? We might be able to change the world one corner at a time. And put the Fart Artists right outta business.

Nobody 101: Whether you are a painter, a baker, a songwriter, or a gardener, see deep anguish as inspiration and turn it into something great.

Somewhere along the line, we've all been taught that if we work hard and do good that it will come back to us. For a lot of Nobodies, this karmic return comes in on a ship that sprang a leak. After a while, we start to think that it must be punishment for our voodoo fantasies involving duct tape.

Where are we for all of our genuine compassion? For putting insects outside instead of in the toilet? For giving our roommate the last cookie in the jar? For cheerleading even our false friends to the finish line? For going easy on the Muttfaces? According to karmic law, it seems our good deeds should pay off in this lifetime, right? Right. Well, they left a very important thing out of the equation: Having compassion means also having compassion for ourselves.

Many of us forget to balance our empathy with self-protection. It doesn't mean we're less caring, less spiritual or less worthy. It simply means that we are no longer pushing all the good stuff away from us because we think someone else might be more deserving.

Walking through the world handing out good will, positivity, support for others, forgiveness and genuine feeling without doing the same for ourselves is like walking through a bad neighborhood decked out in our finest jewels. Sooner or later, we end up with nothing because we never asked for anything else.

Nobody 101: The universe thinks of you exactly how you think of yourself. Give yourself what you give so freely to others and see how fast your ship comes in.

This morning in Nowhere, USA I

noticed a busy squirrel going about his autumnal business, darting from the hickory tree next door to our lawn and then back again. Fifteen minutes later, I noticed the same squirrel pausing in front of our driveway and pondering when he should cross the busy road. One second, two, three…it seemed safe, no cars or sound of engines. The cautious rodent flicked his tail and then scampered to the yellow line. Four quick, disjointed strides before he stopped, hesitated, paused two seconds too long. The sound of gunning engines from both directions filled up the silence. The squirrel twitched with indecision, attempting to finish crossing but turned on a dime when the approaching car barreled down. He headed back toward our house and missed the other car by a hair's width, somersaulting to safety in our driveway. The squirrel swished his tail with flustered dismay, scratched his ear. He then scampered back to the hickory tree without giving the incident a second thought.

I envied that fluffy-tailed, nervous little creature—how he just missed his end by a millisecond, gave himself a moment to freak out and then dusted off the experience like it never happened. If only we were equipped with such instantaneous adaptation.

While I was analyzing this, the squirrel attempted to cross the road again ten minutes later. I held my breath as I watched him. I noticed something different. This time, he didn't pause halfway across but kept moving, keeping his eye on his destination. No nervous flick of tail, no hesitation. Only direct action and utmost confidence.

Nobodies can get to the other side, too, as long as we maintain plenty of agility for all circumstances.

Nobody 101: Snicker at your mishaps, and just keep goin'.

Weeds and the Art of Resilience

If we listen to our own hearts
instead of the Muttface majority, we
are tenacious as weeds. We are
human dandelions who give
naysayers a helluva hard time
stomping us out. Poisonous

indifference, grabbing our self-esteem by the root and inhibiting our growth are only a few Muttface tactics. But there's something in us that refuses to be ignored or destroyed. As long as we don't get caught up in excuses.

We all know life is complicated and busy. We do the 9 to 5, make sure we get the kids off to school and sit through their games, maintain our vanity and do a million other things that go with life in the civilized world. However, if we're dragging our feet when it comes to moving forward with our most treasured plans, we jump on every miniscule reason why we should not or cannot.

Not enough time in the day.

Lack of money.

Aunt Doris needed a pep talk for three hours.

"I'm too old."

The cat has fleas.

Sooner or later, some Nobodies fall into a pattern based on fear of failure. To outside sources, we've been failing every day of our lives and we should just forget the pipe dream. But to ourselves, we know the potential factor, put work into the possibilities and then get cold feet before we see concrete results. That is the exact time when tough self-love has to kick in. Right after we take a nap, have a good cry or scarf down that brownie.

Nobody 101: It takes the same amount of energy to make a decision as it does to make an excuse.

If we wait too long, we start to believe that maybe, just maybe, the Muttfaces are right. We bury the passion and the plans and put our goals on the back burner, in the back of the closet, under the car seat and so far in the back of our minds that we almost believe it's okay for us to live uneventful, lackluster lives.

That's the time we need an honest soul to slap some encouragement into us, a Nobody Caseworker to remind us of our destinies and file the necessary papers to commit us if we don't snap out of temporary insanity. Sometimes that person is nowhere to be seen.

Sometimes, that person has to be the one in the mirror.

101: If you can't find an example, be one.

Despite showing promise at a young age, Nobodies are late bloomers. The road is filled with pot holes, detours, sewer main breaks and 5,000-foot drops without a guard rail. By the time we get to an exit that could actually take us somewhere, we are disheveled, profanity-spewing banshees. It is easy to lose sight of why we started on this road to begin with. It is easy to turn right around and turn on ourselves. If we remain observant, something gets our attention to look at the Big Picture. If we're smart, we remember that destiny is worth waiting for.

Sometimes if we're flexible, the exit leads us to another route and we arrive exactly on time. Our time.

Nobody 101: If the journey isn't joyous, find another road.

Pausing for beauty and gratitude makes the most harrowing journeys worthwhile. Like the flower that is beaten down by wicked weather, we can wear the rain and take jewels from the storm. Our stems and souls are tough. We were also built to soak up today's blessings and make time to live. Making time to live means taking time to notice the view, wearing red in a black and white world and finding the music of our souls beneath the noise. Daydreaming should be on everyone's to-do list.

Nobody 101: Feast on simplicity and revel in possibility. You don't need a perfect life to have a great life.

Whatever brings you bliss, just do it- even if it means making a gourmet dinner for the Muttfaces.

Enjoying the good in life doesn't mean we can ignore the casualties along the way. (No, I wasn't talking about putting poison in that Muttface banquet.) No matter how hard we try, how smart we go about things, how dedicated we are to excellence or how positively we think, we are not immune to ill timing, bad breaks, murdered dreams and unethical Somebodies.

Nobody 101: Watch out for the hyenas. Business is business.

There comes a time when we think we're down for the count. That "they" have won. That the basket we put all of our golden eggs into has been robbed in broad daylight or crushed beneath the screeching tires of reality.

We might check out for a while. Or seal it all in a drawer or burn it to embers. And that's okay. It might take months, years, maybe decades to recover, heal and get our second wind. But it happens. We make it happen.

Nobody 101: Creative energy is infinite. For every withered bloom there are a hundred new possibilities.

Every dark night of the soul has a dawn. The door meant for us is never closed.

MAGIC and HAPPY ENDINGS

A lot of us have had fantasies of
success that include a Muttface
reunion. V.I.P guests such as the
8th grade teacher who accused you
of plagiarism when you wrote a

great book report. Uncle Jasper who said that you never did a lick of "real work" in your life. The successful Somebody who advised you to find another career path... The only problem is that most of them end up kicking the bucket before the day of the banquet, and by the time there is something to celebrate, "showing them all" has lost its appeal because we no longer need validation from other people. Especially those who tried to take it from us to begin with.

For most of us, we unconsciously or consciously gauge our successes by Hollywood standards. After a while, if success doesn't look like a happy ending, we are tricked into the false notion that success is a type of finality. Accomplishment is an ongoing journey—not arriving to a station of wealth (though it would be nice) but a deep and beautiful place of contentment within ourselves. It is a gleaming strand of milestones, one pearl at a time. Milestones are defined by each of us in a different way, and the happiest of us place as much value on the small ones as the big ones.

In the end, success means following your true North wherever it leads you, even if it beckons you to a cabin in the Alaskan wilderness without another human in sight to witness your triumphant arrival. Reaping the harvest of deep accomplishment is hard work because it is authentic work; it is soul-work. And it is magical.

Nobody 101: Magic doesn't just happen- it is made.

This journey of pain and stardust usually comes with an unexpected gift of Self. Who we see in the mirror changes and evolves, and we realize that *what we do matters*, And *this* is the rainbow's end. We might reach that place we're striving for, but the real place of significance turns out to be a state of being, of consciousness, of deep authenticity.

Nobody 101: Reflect your own truth.

Will everyone resonate with your truth? Nope. Will some people resent your truth? Yup. Will there be a high price to pay for living your truth in an insincere world? Maybe. But it's okay. We signed on for the ride knowing everything is worth becoming ourselves.

Nobodies are the cohesive of this world. We heal with our gifts because of, and despite, our wounds. Even the Muttfaces would be lost without us, but don't bother telling them that. Someday, somewhere, it all comes back around.

Well, here in Nowhere, USA I have some things to attend to—simmering plans, impatient dreams and a couple of old demons making themselves comfortable at my kitchen table. All in a day's work for this Nobody. Maybe someday I'll see you at the finish line and we'll go out for a drink. Heck, maybe we'll even buy a round for the Muttfaces.

Nobody 101: The end is only the beginning. Start something wonderful.

Be free!

Index

Nobody 101 Review

...

*Nobody 101: Every Underdog gets his day.

*Nobody 101: Even Muttfaces contribute to our success. They make us want more.

*Nobody 101: Know when to let go...this means attitudes, beliefs, keepsakes, cars, belongings and relationships.

*Nobody 101: Select your free rides carefully.

*Nobody 101: There are good people out there. Don't give up until you find one and then don't screw it up.

*Nobody 101: We all have an inborn right to put our ears back and make our feelings known.

*Nobody 101: Make passion your fuel.

*Nobody 101: Fear can uncover our greatest strengths if we use it to our advantage.

*Nobody 101: Don't get sucked in! If it's *your* ego, stop suckin'.

*Nobody 101: Sometimes not having all the answers is answer enough.

*Nobody 101: Laugh at yourself, even if it kills you.

*Nobody 101: Progress is the only perfection.

*Nobody 101: Refuse to dress, live, or love, according to the whims of the day.

*Nobody 101: Success does not discriminate.

*Nobody 101: Success is seeing what's already been accomplished, not how far you have to go.

*Nobody 101: Choose an honest mountain to climb; all others waste your true purpose.

*Nobody 101: Nothing lasts forever. It's the law of life.

*Nobody 101: Don't apologize for seeing through bullshit.

*Nobody 101: (to quote a fortune cookie) Keep your goals away from the trolls.

*Nobody 101: We were never meant to play small so someone else can feel better.

*Nobody 101: Whether you are a painter, a baker, a songwriter, or a gardener, see deep anguish as inspiration and turn it into something great.

*Nobody 101: The universe thinks of you exactly how you think of yourself. Give yourself what you give so freely

to others and see how fast your ship comes in.

*Nobody 101: Snicker at your mishaps, and just keep goin'.

*Nobody 101: It takes the same amount of energy to make a decision as it does to make an excuse.

*Nobody 101: If you can't find an example, be one.

*Nobody 101: If the journey isn't joyous, find another road.

*Nobody 101: Feast on simplicity and revel in possibility. You don't need a perfect life to have a great life.

*Nobody 101: Watch out for the hyenas. Business is business.

*Nobody 101: Creative energy is infinite. For every withered bloom there are a hundred new possibilities.

*Nobody 101: Magic doesn't just happen- it is made.

*Nobody 101: Reflect your own truth.

*Nobody 101: The end is only the beginning. Start something wonderful.

About the Author

Marlaina Donato came into the world 2 ½ months prematurely, and even her mother had to admit that she looked like a skinny, 2-lb. frog. A late bloomer, she learned to walk and talk at such a late age that it was assumed she would be wearing adult diapers before she was potty trained, which would naturally defeat the purpose. Barely escaping serious bodily harm and permanent insanity, Marlaina dropped out of high school to write, paint and— according to Muttface assumption—live an uneventful, wasted life. Three decades later, she has fourteen books to her name, many plans up her sleeve and the sublime pleasure of living her own brand of success with her wonderful husband, Joe, also an author. **www.marlainadonato.com**

www.ingramcontent.com/pod-product-compliance
Lightning Source LLC
Chambersburg PA
CBHW071822020426
42331CB00007B/1586